WHOSE POO?

POO IN THE JUNGLE

by

Emilie Dufresne

BEARPORT
PUBLISHING

Minneapolis, Minnesota

Credits:

All images are courtesy of Shutterstock.com, unless otherwise specified.
With thanks to Getty Images, Thinkstock Photo, and iStockphoto.

Front Cover - PremiumVector, ainahart, Iakov Filimonov, Iterum, YevO, Iron 2016, Valeri Hadeev.
Title typeface used throughout - PremiumVector, vector flies - Top Vector Studio. 2 - Chadchai
Krisadapong, Anne Punch, Indayani, 4-5 - Maquiladora, THRUS PANYAWACHIROPAS, Freebird7977,
6-7 - yekaterinalim, Nathapol Kongseang, Dirk Ercken, Anan Kaewkhammul, 8-9 - MAHATHIR
MOHD YASIN, belizar, SaveJungle, 10-11 - Anand Osuri (wiki commons), Anan Kaewkhammul, Anna.
zabella, Eric Isselee, somsak mungmee, 12-13 - svtdesign, cosmaa, Anna Violet, Mazur Travel,
Rbalmonia (wiki commons), Mary Valery, 14-15 - apple2499, Eric Isselee, HappyPictures, Kakigori
Studio, Twan Bankers, 16-17 - Oleh Dovhan, Thorsten Spoerlein, Shahril KHMD, 18-19 - Creativa
Images, Eric Isselee, imaginasty, Vladyslav Severyn, Cayce (wiki commons), 20-21 - Kastoluza,
Bill Roque, jeep2499, aelitta, 22-23 - sjdross75, "sloth" flickr photo by davida3
https://flickr.com/photos/davida3/417503724 shared under a Creative Commons (BY-ND) license.

Library of Congress Cataloging-in-Publication Data

Names: Dufresne, Emilie, author.
Title: Poo in the jungle / by Emilie Dufresne.
Description: Fusion. | Minneapolis, Minnesota : Bearport Publishing, [2021]
   | Series: Whose poo? | Includes bibliographical references and index.
Identifiers: LCCN 2020009337 (print) | LCCN 2020009338 (ebook) | ISBN
   9781647473846 (library binding) | ISBN 9781647473891 (paperback) | ISBN
   9781647473945 (ebook)
Subjects: LCSH: Jungles–Juvenile literature. | Feces–Juvenile literature.
Classification: LCC QH86 .D843 2021 (print) | LCC QH86 (ebook) | DDC
   577.34–dc23
LC record available at https://lccn.loc.gov/2020009337
LC ebook record available at https://lccn.loc.gov/2020009338

For more information, write to Bearport Publishing, 5357 Penn Avenue South, Minneapolis, MN 55419. Printed in the
United States of America.

CONTENTS

ALL ABOUT POO

What's that smell? Did you step in something? Oh no! It's poo! But who made it? Let's look around the jungle and find out.

An animal's poo tells you a lot about them!

Sniff!
Sniff!

Don't touch poo you find in the jungle. Poo has lots of nasty things in it!

On the next pages, you will see poo in the jungle. Learn all about the poo and think about which animal made it. Then, turn the page to see if you were right!

A BIG SPLAT

Wow—look at this watery poo! Whose poo could it be?

This poo has splattered. The animal must have pooed from high up.

This poo looks like a liquid. This animal probably doesn't eat solid food.

Splash!

Splash!

6

Whose poo could this be? Choose which of these three animals you think made the poo.

Liquid diet? I don't think so! Where's my meat?

Jaguar

This poo is in a jungle cave. The animal probably lives in the cave.

Vampire bat

There are other splats of poo around this one. This animal probably lives in a big group.

Frog

7

WHOSE POO WAS IT?

It was the vampire bat's POO!

What are you looking at?

Vampire bats feed only on the blood of other animals. This means their poo is totally wet.

Everyone get out of the way—I need to poo!

Not again, Lucy!

Vampire bats live in big groups. Their cave floors are often covered in poo splats.

Vampire bats drink about two tablespoons of blood every day. They usually poo it out after only two minutes.

9

FULL OF BEANS

What a strange-looking poo! Whose could it be?

This poo has a lot of seeds in it. This animal must eat lots of berries.

Pee-yew! This poo is very smelly. The bad smell may be a way to communicate with other animals.

Choose which of these three animals you think pooed out all those seeds.

The seeds in this poo are from berries only found in the branches of trees. So, this animal must be a climber.

Whoa, that stinks! I hope it wasn't me.

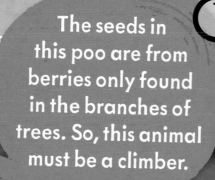

This is a big pile of poo. This animal probably uses a shared toilet.

Civet

Tapir

Piranha

WHOSE POO WAS IT?

It was the **civet's POO!**

My poo might smell, but at least it's worth a lot of money....

Civets mostly live alone, but they will share places to poo with other civets.

Some civets eat coffee cherries that contain seeds. The seeds can't be **digested**, so they come out in poo!

These seeds are used to make coffee. Some people think this poo coffee tastes better than normal coffee!

One cup of this coffee can cost up to $100! That's a lot of money for a hot cup of poo!

13

SERIOUSLY SMELLY

What a large and stinky poo! What kind of animal could have done this?

This poo has a very strong smell to it.

This poo has hair in it. This animal probably eats other animals.

WHOSE POO WAS IT?

It was the **tiger's** POO!

Sniff, sniff! I don't think it smells that bad.

16

The fur that tigers eat can't be digested, so it comes out in their poo. This tells us what animals the tigers have been eating.

Tigers give off a powerful smell when they poo. This helps them mark their **territory**.

Tigers poo so much that a tiger mother might eat her cubs' poo so other **predators** won't smell it

Thanks, Mom...and sorry!

GRASSY AND SEEDY

Another poo! Whose poo could this be?

This poo has **vegetation** in it. This animal probably eats plants.

Which of these three animals do you think made this poo?

Come on, guys! Everyone does it!

The poo also has seeds in it. This animal probably likes to eat fruit found high up in jungle trees.

There are insect parts in this poo. The animal must eat both plants and animals.

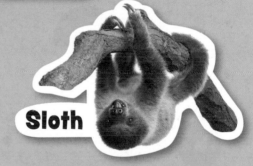
Orangutan

Sloth

Leopard

19

WHOSE POO WAS IT?

It was the
orangutan's
POO!

I ate all the fruit and then made the poo!

The seeds of the fruit that orangutans eat can't be digested, so they come out in their poo. One orangutan poo was found that had 828 seeds in it!

Orangutans are called gardeners of the jungle because the seeds in their poo help new plants grow in the jungles.

If there isn't enough fruit, orangutans will eat leaves, twigs, bark, and even insects.

Orangutans sometimes use leaves as toilet paper.

21

BONUS POO!

THE SLOWEST POO ON EARTH?

It is not surprising that one of the slowest creatures on Earth also takes a long time to poo. It can take a sloth a whole month to digest its food.

I take my time!

Sloths only poo once a week! Unlike other animals who live in trees, sloths poo on the ground. This means they have to climb down and look out for predators while they poo.

A sloth can lose up to one-third of its weight when it poos.

Hey, a little privacy please!

GLOSSARY

communicate to pass information between two or more things

diet the kinds of food that a person or animal usually eats

digested to have broken down food into things that can be used by the body

liquid a thing that flows, such as water

predators animals that hunt other animals for food

solid firm and stable

territory the area where an animal lives and finds its food

vegetation different types of plants, including grass, bushes, and trees

INDEX